<u>INDEX</u>

Back in 2003

Following Iran's apparent role in kick-starting the long-delayed formation of a government in Baghdad, Tehran is seen by many as the most influential external power in Iraq. While this may or may not be true, it is clear that Iran has a proven ability to commission violence inside Iraq. Yet while the covert programs run by the Iranian Revolutionary Guard Corps (IRGC) Qods Force is a source of influence in Iraq, paramilitary operations come at a cost. The militarization of Iranian influence is often counterproductive in Iraq, reinforcing Iraqis' generally negative attitudes toward Iran. Tehran's concern about negative Iraqi perceptions of its paramilitary proxies has influenced the evolution of Iranian support to the so-called "Special Groups" of militant Shi`a diehards in Iraq.

The Islamic Republic of Iran has been in the business of sponsoring Iraqi paramilitary proxies for 30 years, practically the government's entire existence. In some cases, the same Iraqi individuals run like a thread throughout the entire story, from Islamic terrorists, to exiled anti-Saddam guerrillas, to anti-American Special Group fighters in post-Ba`athist Iraq. Many of the historical patterns of Iranian support to Iraqi proxies hold true today.

Although paramilitary action is just one strand of Iranian influence-building in Iraq, it plays a particularly important role in Iran's pursuit of security-related objectives. As well as seeking to hasten the U.S. withdrawal, the Special Groups demonstrate Iran's ability to destabilize Iraq. More broadly, the Special Groups represent a flexible tool that might be used to aid Iran's effort to prevent nationalist and former Ba`athists from rising to the top of Iraqi politics and to maintain leverage over a new Shi`a-led government.

According to pre-2003 Iraqi government reporting on Iranian proxy operations, the IRGC Qods Force had already anticipated the need to split its support between groups that would "work openly" and others that would "work secretly" in a post-invasion Iraq. Ba`athist reporting appears to have been well-sourced and accurate in many respects: they correctly anticipated Iran's ability to support public organizations such as the Islamic Supreme Council of Iraq (ISCI) and the paramilitary Badr Organization, while also backing covert Special

Groups. A consistent feature of Iran's patronage has been careful efforts to spread Tehran's bets across many different horses.

Special Group Operations

The armed factions that make up the Special Groups have passed through significant changes in the last years, and they continue to evolve. The government security offensives of spring 2008 caused considerable damage to Iranian-backed networks, and many Special Group operators fled to sanctuaries in Iran. Since the summer of 2009, these groups have been allowed breathing space to recover and begin to reestablish their presence in Iraq.

There are many reasons why recovery has been possible. In June 2009, the U.S.-Iraq security agreement ended the ability of U.S. forces to operate unilaterally in Iraq's cities, where much of the fight against the Special Groups has been conducted. The U.S. military thereafter required an Iraqi warrant and Iraqi military cooperation to undertake raids against the Special Groups. In the extended lead-up to Iraq's March 2010 elections, Prime Minister Nuri al-Maliki sought to win favor with other Shi`a factions by using his direct operational control of Iraq's Counterterrorism Command to place a virtual embargo on such raids. Lacking the judicial evidence to hold Special Group detainees transferred to the Iraqi government, and facing pressure from Shi`a groups, the government began to release Special Group prisoners as soon as they were transferred to Iraqi custody by the United States. The military cells supported by Iran are spread across the legal spectrum, from completely covert organizations to political parties with deniable connections to the IRGC Qods Force.

Iran's Changed Approach

The period since 2003 has witnessed a balance of Iranian successes and failures in its proxy operations in Iraq. On the one hand, Iran has kept up military pressure on U.S. forces in Iraq and has demonstrated its ability to destabilize key areas. On the other hand, Iranian paramilitary involvement in Iraq is widely resented by Iraqis and has contributed to the downturn in the political fortunes of pro-Iranian parties such as the ISCI, driving other Shi`a blocs (such as al-Maliki's Da`wa Party) to distance themselves from Iran.

This trend was most clear in the early months of 2007 when Iran's political allies in Iraq issued a demarche to the IRGC Qods Force to scale back its support of Iraqi militias. After Lebanese Hezbollah's successful "summer war" against Israel in July 2006, the IRGC Qods Force sought to replicate this victory in Iraq, opening the floodgates to provide advanced Explosively-Formed Projectile (EFP) munitions and other weapons to a wide range of Shi`a Islamist factions. The result was internecine assassinations of two provincial governors and two provincial police chiefs in the latter half of 2006, all Shi`a-on-Shi`a political killings using EFPs. The IRGC resolved to narrow its support for groups to more trusted entities after rival Shia groups began fighting in the shrine city of Karbala in late August 2007, which was the final straw for Iraq's Shi`a political and religious leaders.

The re-think of Iranian support to Iraqi militants has had far-reaching effects. The development of alternatives to the out-of-control Jaysh al-Mahdi is one reason why new formations such as KH and AAH were developed. The need to place Iraqis in leadership roles is another factor, reflecting arrests of IRGC personnel in Iraq in 2005-2007, which showed that it was too risky to deploy significant numbers of Iranian IRGC personnel or even Lebanese Hezbollah operatives to Iraq.

According to U.S. and Iraqi security force interviewees, the IRGC Qods Force centralized its resupply operations to KH and AAH cells, adding a system of accounting for Iranian-supplied weapons. This meant moving from the "pull" system—where Iraqis came to ask a cell leader for weapons—to a more secure and selective "push" system, where the cell leader would allocate weapons to well-paid and experienced fighters who were known to be reliable. Each major arms cache now has a "hide custodian" who signs out weapons such as EFPs and is responsible for their proper use against U.S. forces and the minimization of Iraqi casualties. Money continues to be provided in significant volumes, allowing cells to be paid between $4,000 and $13,000 per rocket or roadside bomb attack, depending on the circumstances. Communications security and operational security are aided by the compact size of cells.

A constant feature of Iran's policy for more than 20 years has been the importance of uninterrupted cross-border resupply for Iran's proxies in Iraq. The broad outlines of cross-border movement have not changed greatly from the early 1990s in many places. The general principle is that personnel and equipment move through official points of entry (POE) whenever possible. For personnel, this is almost always possible due to the primitiveness of Iraq's customs and immigration services and due to the combined effects of corruption and professionally-forged documentation. Until the introduction of U.S.-provided vehicle scanning equipment, the Special Groups could bring weapons and explosives into Iraq through the POE on flatbed trucks, concealed beneath herds of sheep or bags of cement. Even now, corruption and the slow degradation of the equipment make it possible to use border crossings to bring specialized equipment such as the milled copper cones for EFP munitions into the country.

The use of professional smugglers is an age-old Iranian practice, involving cross-border tribes and corrupt border guards. Smuggling boats make daylight transits of the Hawr al-Howeiza, marshes in Maysan Province, with rockets and other equipment concealed under tarpaulins covered with fishing gear and fresh fish. On land, the key routes continue to be the Badra area of Wasit Province, the northern Maysan border at multiple points, and eastern Basra (south of Majnoon and north of Shalamcheh). Iran's armed forces support border crossings with a number of means, including use of its own unmanned aerial vehicles, helicopters, long-range optics, signals intelligence and intimidation firing to discourage Iraqi border guard patrolling.

The sophistication of indirect fire attacks is also increasing. In Baghdad and other cities, Special Groups tend to make greater use of 60mm and 81mm mortars to precisely target small U.S. Joint Security Stations. Banks of Improvised Rocket-Assisted Mortars (IRAM) have been used to great effect against urban U.S. bases in Baghdad and Amara. Efforts have also been made to increase the effectiveness of rocket attacks by launching horizontally at close range from within parked vehicles, launching at shallow angles to reduce warning and prevent interception by close-in weapons systems, or by overwhelming defenses with salvoes of 16-20 truck-launched rockets. Although indirect fire attacks are largely a harassment weapon, they have caused five fatalities to U.S. personnel and contractors in the last year.

The other visible sign of Special Group activity are roadside bombs. At present, these are almost entirely targeted on U.S. military vehicles plus the distinctive personal security detail vehicles that service U.S. reconstruction officials (which carry electronic countermeasures not seen on other vehicles). As a signature weapon for Iranian-backed groups, EFPs are employed carefully to reduce Iraqi casualties. Due to this restriction plus the reduced number of U.S. targets on Iraq's roads, the incidence of EFP use has dropped from around 60 per month at the height of the "surge" in 2007 to an average of 17 per month in the first nine months of 2010. To access U.S. targets, EFP cells have activated in areas where they were previously rarely encountered such as in Abu Ghurayb, Khalis and Muqdadiyya (in Diyala Province), and Kirkuk.

Per incident lethality has declined significantly since 2008 due to U.S. countermeasures and less effective weapons assembly and emplacement capabilities. Sporadic shortfalls in EFP components are apparent in the varying sophistication and composition of devices. Iranian-made C4, identifiable through chemical analysis, is less frequently used in EFPs today; more often the main charge is composed of five to 40 pounds of unidentified bulk explosive. The EFP "liners" (the metal cone used to form the penetrator) come in up to a dozen sizes, with diameters between 2.75 inches and 16 inches. The liners are largely better-quality copper cones, although some steel liners are used and some multiple-array devices have included a mix of copper and steel liners.

Despite the downscaling of EFP operations, the "engineer" cells capable of assembling EFPs and mounting such attacks continue to show signs of adaptation. Cells in Basra, Baghdad and along the main Supply Route Tampa South (between Baghdad and the Kuwaiti border) switch attack sites to match the movement patterns of U.S. units. The cells attempt to overcome U.S. countermeasures by offsetting the aiming points for devices (to take into account the "rhino" booms on U.S. vehicles), angling devices upwards to strike windows, and elevating devices up lampposts and within T-walls or abandoned checkpoints to avoid the booms.

Cells also show adaptability in their combination of EFP elements (such as passive infrared firing switches) with claymore-style direction fragmentation charges. Large-caliber "daisy-chained" artillery shells (122mm to 155mm) are also periodically used to target U.S. vehicles. The highest quality Special Group bomb-maker cells active in Iraq appear to be based in northern Baghdad, Basra and in the Suq ash Shuyukh area, a marshland market town east of Nasiriyya that was a Badr stronghold throughout the Saddam era and a notorious den of thieves for hundreds of years before then.

A final and even murkier aspect of the Special Groups is their involvement with the deliberate killings of Iraqis. In the past, this aspect of Special Group activity has brought significant criticism onto Iran and its proxies. Although some Iraqis are killed in Special Group operations (as unintended civilian deaths in rocket or roadside bombing attacks or Iraqi Army deaths when joint U.S.-Iraqi patrols are bombed), deliberate targeting of Iraqis appears to be rare and selective.

Evidence from arms caches suggests that Iranian-backed groups that stockpile EFP components and other Iranian signature weapons (240mm rockets, for instance) also maintain stocks of silenced pistols and under-vehicle magnetic IEDs ("sticky bombs"). These assassination tools suggest that some "direct action" is still undertaken against Iraqis to serve the political agenda of Iranian proxies or Iran's direct interests, or that such action could be undertaken again in the future.

Quds Force

The Quds Force has been around since the 1980s, and their biggest success has been in Lebanon, where they helped local Shia (who comprise about a third of the population) form the Hezbollah organization. After 2003 Quds Force helped Hezbollah create Unit 3800 to help train Islamic radical Shia militias in Iraq. These militias were frequently used to attack American troops as well as Sunni Islamic terrorists. Unit 3800 personnel were easier to hide since they were Arabs while most of the Quds people are ethnic Iranian (Indo-European) and have a hard time passing for Arabs,

The Quds Force, being a much larger organization than Unit 3800, also has a lot more responsibilities. Thus Quds has eight departments, each assigned to a different part of the world. While the one that works in the Palestine/Lebanon/Jordan area have been the most successful, the other departments have been hard at it for over two decades. Quds Force also helped Hezbollah create Unit 1800, whose main function is to help train Palestinian Islamic terrorists.

The Western Directorate has established a recruiting and fund raising network in Western nations. Many recruits are brought back to Iran for training, while Shia migrants are encouraged to donate money, and services, to Quds Force operations. Because many of these operations are considered terrorist operations, Quds Force is banned in many Western nations.

The Iraq Department long maintained an army of anti-Saddam fighters in exile (in Iran) as well as running an intelligence operation inside Iraq. After the coalition toppled Saddam in 2003, Quds Force moved people, money and weapons into Iraq, to form pro-Iranian political forces and militias. These are the men withdrawn after 2008 and who are back now.

The South Asia Department (Afghanistan, Pakistan, and India) was active in aiding Afghan Shia who were being persecuted by the Taliban (a Sunni operation) and al Qaeda (a very Sunni operation). Quds has also been caught operating in Pakistan, where Sunni terrorists have been attacking Shia for decades.

The Turkey Department has been active encouraging Shia Kurds to commit terrorist acts.

The North Africa Department has an operation in Sudan that functions in the open despite the Sunni conservatives who run the country. This department was caught providing weapons to the Sunni Islamic Courts militia in Somalia in 2007 and later providing support for the even more radical al Shabaab.

The Arabian Department supports terrorist groups that exist in all the Persian Gulf Arab countries. The Arab Sunni governments in these nations does not appreciate Iran's support for this sort of thing.

The Central Asian Department supports Shia and Sunni terrorists in countries that used to be part of the Soviet Union. So does al Qaeda, but the Quds operation has been more discreet.

Back in Iran, Quds is believed to provide safe houses (or house arrest) for al Qaeda and other Sunni Islamic terrorist leaders, even though al Qaeda has taken part in many atrocities against Shia outside Iran. However, the "enemy of my enemy is my friend." Actually, there is an ongoing dispute in the Iranian government over the al Qaeda issue. But the Iranian leadership is more a federation than a dictatorship, so Quds can keep being nice to al Qaeda as long as not too many factions get mad at Quds.

The Iranian leadership, despite their radical sounding pronouncements, have actually been quite cautious. This is in line with ancient Iranian custom. Most of the Hezbollah violence in Lebanon was at the behest of Lebanese. The same pattern has occurred elsewhere. The Quds guys usually counsel restraint, although in Iraq there has been more enthusiasm for violence. Iraq is a special case, as several hundred thousand Iranians died fighting Saddam in the 1980s, and Iranians have not forgotten. While Saddam is dead and gone many of his followers are in ISIL and for the Iranians the debt is still not paid.

Kataib Hezbollah

Kataib Hezbollah (KH) was formed in early 2007 as a vehicle through which the IRGC Qods Force could deploy its most experienced operators and its most sensitive equipment. Much can be gleaned from the positioning of Abu Mahdi al-Muhandis (whose real name is Jamal al-Ibrahimi) as the leader of KH. Born in Basra, al-Muhandis is an adviser to IRGC Qods Force commander Qasem Soleimani.

The life history of al-Muhandis describes the arc of Iranian support for Iraqi Shi`a proxies, with al-Muhandis starting as an exiled member of the outlawed Da`wa Party, working with the IRGC Qods Force to undertake terrorist operations against the Kuwaiti royal family and the U.S. and French embassies in Kuwait in the early 1980s. Al-Muhandis then joined the Badr movement while living in Iran in 1985, rising to become one of the Iraqi deputy commanders of Badr by 2001. He is a strategist with extensive experience dealing directly with the most senior Iraqi politicians; indeed, al-Muhandis was, until the March 2010 elections, an elected member of parliament, albeit spending most of his time in Iran. Under al-Muhandis, KH has developed as a compact movement of less than 400 personnel that is firmly under IRGC Qods Force control and maintains relatively good operational security.

Asaib Ahl al-Haq

Asaib Ahl al-Haq (AAH) emerged between 2006 and 2008 as part of an effort by the IRGC Qods Force to create a popular organization similar to Lebanese Hezbollah that would be easier to shape than Moqtada al-Sadr's uncontrollable Jaysh al-Mahdi (JAM) movement. AAH was built around one of al-Sadr's key rivals, a protégé of al-Sadr's father called Qais al-Khazali who had consistently opposed al-Sadr's cease-fire agreements with the U.S. and Iraqi militaries. After AAH undertook the kidnap and murder of five U.S. soldiers on January 20, 2007, al-Khazali was captured by coalition forces alongside his brother Laith Khazali and Lebanese Hezbollah operative Ali Musa Daqduq in Basra on March 20, 2007.

In time, al-Khazali was transferred to Iraqi custody and then released in exchange for kidnapped Briton Peter Moore on January 5, 2010. Although far less senior in the IRGC Qods Force hierarchy than al-Muhandis and 20 years his junior, Qais al-Khazali could become a significant political force in mainstream politics and is being courted by both al-Maliki and al-Sadr precisely because he has the capability to draw away a portion of Moqtada's supporters if he so chooses.

During al-Khazali's absence in prison, AAH played a delicate game, balancing the need to negotiate for the release of detainees against the desire of many AAH members to continue attacking U.S. forces. Like its predecessor, Jaysh al-Mahdi, AAH is becoming a catch-all for a wide range of militants who seek to engage in violence for a host of ideological, sectarian or purely commercial motives. Notorious Special Group commanders such as Sadrist breakaway Abu Mustapha al-Sheibani (whose real name is Hamid Thajeel al-Sheibani) and infamous Shi`a warlord Abu Deraa (whose real name is Ismail al-Lami) are reported to be returning from Iran to join AAH.

Promised Day Brigades

The Promised Day Brigades (PDB) are the least understood of the major Iranian-influenced Shi`a militant groups. In theory, PDB is a Shi`a nationalist militia that provides Moqtada al-Sadr's militant followers a way to justify staying within his organization while reserving the theoretical right to fight U.S. forces. In practice, many purported members of PDB appear to collaborate with KH and AAH organizers to participate in small numbers of attacks on U.S. forces.

Badr Organization

Although the Badr Organization is a major political organization with seats in the new parliament, it also arguably plays a significant role in facilitating Special Group operations in Iraq. When it was formed in the early 1980s, the Badr movement was, in effect, the first Special Group. A proportion of senior Special Group commanders such as Abu Mahdi al-Muhandis are Badr personnel, with long-standing ties to current Badr leader Hadi al-Amiri. After 2003, Badr became the part of the IRGC Qods Force that was selected to "work openly" within the new Iraq. Badr inserted hundreds of its Iranian-trained operatives into the state security organs (notably the Ministry of Interior intelligence structure and key special forces and Iraqi Army units). As a result, the Special Groups have regularly received tip-offs and targeting guidance from their "fellow travelers" in the Badr movement.

Outlook for the Special Groups

The political situation in Iraq will have a significant effect on the further evolution of Special Groups. If, as seems likely, Moqtada al-Sadr joins key Iranian-backed parties such as Badr in the new government, many elements of PDB, AAH and KH will probably be drawn into the security forces as Badr personnel were in the post-2003 period. Some types of violence (such as rocketing of the government center in Baghdad) may decline, while targeted attacks on U.S. forces would persist or even intensify due to the new latitude enjoyed by such groups.

Kidnap of Western contractors or military personnel has been the subject of government warnings during 2010 and could become a significant risk if U.S.-Iran tensions increase in coming years. Sectarian utilization of the Special Groups to target Sunni nationalist oppositionists could become a problem once again. If Iraqi government policy crosses any "red lines" (such as long-term U.S. military presence in Iraq, rapid rearmament or anti-Iranian oil policy), the Special Groups could be turned against the Iraqi state in service of Iranian interests, showering the government center with rockets or assassinating key individuals.

As has been shown throughout the Islamic Republic of Iran's 30-year engagement in Iraq, however, other Iraqi militant groups will continue to chart their own course and will make and break cease-fires according to their own interests.

Nasrallah goes to ...Bagdad

As Sunni militants from the Islamic State of Iraq and al-Sham (ISIS) captured Mosul, Nasrallah offered to send fighters to Iraq to help turn the jihadist tide. In Syria, the Lebanese Shiite group's forces have already deployed in large numbers over the past several years and made all the difference in the Assad regime's battle for survival. In Iraq, Hezbollah would likely dispatch only small numbers of trainers and special operators. Yet given the group's past special operations and training activities in Iraq and its close ties with Iran's elite Qods Force, even a modest deployment would likely have a significant impact.

On June 17, Nasrallah pledged, "We are ready to sacrifice martyrs in Iraq five times more than what we sacrificed in Syria in order to protect shrines," noting that Iraqi holy sites "are much more important" than Shiite shrines in Syria. To be sure, Hezbollah is heavily invested in the Syria war and will probably increase its presence there as Iraqi Shiites leave to defend their homeland from ISIS. Yet the group can make a significant contribution to the Shiite counteroffensive in Iraq without having to redirect many of its operatives or resources from Syria.

During the last Iraq war, Hezbollah effectively used a limited number of special operations personnel to train Iraqi Shiite militants and support sporadic special operations targeting coalition forces. As a 2009 Australian government report concluded, "*Hezbollah has established an insurgent capability in Iraq, engaging in assassinations, kidnappings and bombings. The Hezbollah units have been set up with the encouragement and resources of Iran's Revolutionary Guards al-Qods Brigades.*" The Qods Force will likely request a similar initiative to aid the Shiite-led government in Baghdad today, turning these capabilities against ISIS with potentially far-reaching benefits for Iraqi Shiite militias.

Beginning in 2003, Iran's Qods Force requested Hezbollah's services to help increase Tehran's influence in Iraq. To this end, Hezbollah created Unit 3800, whose sole purpose was to support Iraqi Shiite militant groups targeting multinational forces there. According to U.S. intelligence, Unit 3800 sent a small number of personnel to Iraq to train hundreds of fighters in-country, while others were brought to Lebanon for more advanced training. Hezbollah also provided funds and weapons to Iraqi militias, but its most dangerous contribution was in the realm of special operations.

According to a 2010 Pentagon report, the group gave these militias "*the training, tactics and technology to conduct kidnappings [and] small unit tactical operations,*" and to "*employ sophisticated improvised explosive devices (IEDs), incorporating lessons learned from operations in Southern Lebanon.*"

The most prominent example of how this training helped the militias was probably the January 20, 2007, attack on the Joint Coordination Center in Karbala, which resulted in the deaths of four American soldiers. That well-executed operation was thoroughly planned with the help of the Qods Force and Hezbollah, as determined later through the capture of one of Hezbollah's best trainers in Iraq, Ali Musa Daqduq.

Daqduq was heavily involved in training tactical units of Iraqi Shiites and even took part in some of the operations they conducted. He was also responsible for planning other operations such as the aborted kidnapping of a British soldier, and gave specific instructions to those he trained about the use of IEDs. Moreover, while operating in Iraq, he dealt directly with the Qods Force on certain occasions -- further evidence of the high level of coordination between Hezbollah and the Iranians on Iraq.

Since American and multinational forces withdrew from Iraq, Unit 3800 has been put to work elsewhere in the region, primarily in Yemen. There, Hezbollah and Qods Force personnel have helped the Houthis, a Zaidi Shiite insurgent group, fight the government. Reports from the Treasury Department and the New York Times indicate that Hezbollah and Qods personnel coordinated their operations in Yemen, with the former in charge of transferring funds and training Shiite insurgents, and the latter in charge of transferring advanced weapons such as antiaircraft missiles. U.S. intelligence agencies detected these activities, which led former White House counterterrorism advisor John Brennan to state in October 2012, "*We have seen Hezbollah training militants in Yemen and Syria.*" National Intelligence Director James Clapper reinforced this point in his January 2014 "Worldwide Threat Assessment," noting that "*Iran will continue to provide arms and other aid to Palestinian groups, [Houthi] rebels in Yemen, and Shia militants in Bahrain to expand Iranian influence and to counter perceived foreign threats.*"

Besides branching out to Yemen, Unit 3800 received another boost to its capabilities and prestige in 2012, when Hajj Khalil Harb -- a longtime Hezbollah commander and close advisor to Nasrallah -- was appointed to lead it. Harb is an experienced operative who has held various key positions, especially in terms of working with other terrorist organizations and overseeing special operations. He served as deputy commander of Hezbollah's central military unit in Southern Lebanon during the late 1980s, where he gained his first substantial experience in special operations against Israeli forces. He later assumed command of Unit 1800, the Hezbollah force dedicated to assisting Palestinian terrorist groups by operating in the "ring countries" around Israel and infiltrating individuals into Israeli territory to conduct terrorist attacks and collect intelligence. According to the Treasury Department, Harb also traveled to Iran many times in his role as coordinator between Hezbollah, the Palestinians, and Tehran. After his role in Yemen became apparent to U.S. intelligence, the department designated him for sanctions in August 2013, citing his long body of work.

Appointing Harb to head Unit 3800 no doubt made a great deal of sense to Hezbollah's leaders given his experience working with other terrorist organizations, his close relations with the Iranians, and his expertise in special operations and training. The unit has likely benefited from his guidance and upgraded its capabilities since then. Deploying members of this unit to Iraq would also make sense given Harb's status as a former advisor to Nasrallah, who would presumably want an experienced commander in charge of such an important arena.

The war in Syria requires a great commitment from Hezbollah in terms of personnel and weapons, and significant numbers of its fighters have already lost their lives in helping the Assad regime. Yet given its willingness to answer Iran's call for help in Syria, the group will probably answer the call to fight in Iraq as well. Nasrallah is already laying the groundwork to justify such involvement by invoking the same hollow excuse of "defending Shiites and Shiite holy places." As in the past, Hezbollah's contribution does not have to include hundreds of fighters, but only a limited number of experienced trainers and special operations "consultants." This type of contribution would not overstrain the organization, and it could facilitate far-reaching achievements for Iraqi Shiite militias.

Hezbollah's past operations in Iraq show that a limited number of experienced "consultants," working with Iran's Qods Force, could significantly increase the lethality of the local Shiite militias currently gearing up to counter the ISIS offensive.

Visibility on Lebanese Hezbollah's current response to the crisis in Iraq has markedly increased, with reliable sources describing that military advisors are being deployed from Lebanon to assist Iraqi Shi'a militia forces. Sources close to Hezbollah have revealed that a 250-member advisory unit is being deployed to Iraq. The unit's primary mission is to advise, train, and coordinate Iraqi Shi'a militias operating under the guidance of Iran's Islamic Revolutionary Guard Corps (IRGC). The sources furthermore indicated that the advisory unit is also already engaged in conducting intelligence and reconnaissance operations against ISIS forces. This advisory mission echoes Hezbollah's early primary role in Syria as advisers and trainers of pro-regime forces.

Unit 3800

Operating in Iraq is nothing new to Hezbollah. In approximately 2005, Iran requested that Hezbollah stand up a group to support the training and operations of the Mahdi Army and the Special Groups in Iraq. The resulting organization was Hezbollah's Unit 3800 (earlier known as Unit 2800), designed to supplant ongoing advisory efforts to Iraqi Shi'a militias being undertaken by Department 9000 of the IRGC-Qods Force's (IRGC-QF) Ramazan Corps. Unit 3800 drew on expertise from Hezbollah's Unit 1800, which provides support to Palestinian militant groups such as Hamas, as well as Hezbollah's own special operations community.

The Lebanese Unit 3800 is modeled on the Iranian Quds Force. Both are full time operations, composed of men trained to spread the Islamic revolution outside Iran. The core operatives of the Quds force comprises only a few thousand people. Unit 3800 is much smaller, with only a few hundred members. But many of these operatives are highly educated, most speak foreign languages, and all are Islamic radicals. They are on a mission from God to convert the world to Shia Islam, and the rule of Shia clergy.

According to a 2010 Defense Intelligence Agency report, Department 9000 and Unit 3800 were providing *"the training, tactics, and technology to conduct kidnappings, small unit tactical operations, and employ sophisticated improvised explosive devices (IEDs)."* From 2003 to 2005, Hezbollah's primary engagement was with the Mahdi Army; after the Special Groups emerged in 2006, they became the primary recipients of Unit 3800's attention. In 2007, with rising tensions between local Iraqi Shi'a and Iranian trainers alongside marked Coalition pressure on IRGC activities in-country, Unit 3800 more and more became the Arab intermediary for Iranian support to Iraqi Shia militias. By 2008, it was reported that Hezbollah's Secretary-General Hassan Nasrallah was spending "several hours" a day on matters related to Iraq.

Unit 3800 conducted training missions in Iraq, Lebanon, and Iran – while also supporting actual militia operations. Unit 3800 trainer and Hezbollah liaison to

IRGC Ali Musa Daqduq, who was in custody from 2007 to 2012 before being released by Iraqi authorities, was tied to the January 20, 2007 attack on the Joint Coordination Center in Karbala, which resulted in the abduction and murder of four American soldiers. That attack was carried out by Qais al-Khazali's Iranian-sponsored Asa'ib Ahl al-Haq (AAH) and later linked to Abdul Reza Shahlai, the Deputy Commander of IRGC-QF Special External Operations Unit. Evidence also exists that Hezbollah may have been conducting its own operations in Iraq as well. When conducting operations outside of Lebanon, Hezbollah has traditionally relied on its feared External Security Organization (ESO), which is responsible for both terror operations abroad and contributes to some intelligence and special operations. If Hezbollah was operating in Iraq beyond providing training, it is likely that ESO members were taking part.

Since the departure of Coalition forces from Iraq, Unit 3800 commander Khalil Harb has been spotted in Yemen in 2012 and then-U.S. Homeland Security Advisor John Brennan described Hezbollah as "training militants in Yemen." Unit 3800's presence was likely in support of ongoing Iranian assistance to Houthi rebels there. The training requirements of Houthi groups are more conventional than the special operations-oriented training provided to the Special Groups. Thus, between missions in Yemen and the ongoing training of Iraqi Shi'a militias for action in Syria, Unit 3800 has likely developed a more sophisticated and multifaceted training capacity by drawing on both Hezbollah's more conventional infantry experts and special operators, such as those from the ESO.

Elite trainers from Hezbollah, such as those fielded by Unit 3800, have also played a major role in Iran's assistance to the Syrian regime. While Hezbollah's support to the Assad regime is clearly multifaceted, trainers in particular have played a major role in contributing to force integration between pro-Assad militias, Iraqi Shi'a militants in Syria, and the Syrian military. Hezbollah's combat operations in Syria have also produced a new generation of experienced fighters on which it can draw.

Hezbollah, alongside Iraqi Shi'a militias that have deployed to Syria, are components of an "Axis of Resistance" that have shown the ability to operate together in multiple theaters. It is telling that Muhammad Kawtharani, who as of 2013 was Hezbollah's manager of all Iraqi operations, has assisted in coordinating the movement of Hezbollah fighters to support pro-regime forces in Syria. It would be unsurprising for Kawtharani to be involved in Hezbollah's renewed deployment to Iraq.

On June 29, Brigadier General Massoud Jazayeri, deputy joint chief of staff of the Iranian armed forces and a senior IRGC officer, announced that *"the same winning strategy used in Syria to put the terrorists on the defensive … is now taking shape in Iraq."* Given Hezbollah's experience, it is quite possible that the new advisory unit in Iraq will play a similar force integration role in working to coordinate between the Iraqi military and Iraqi Shi'a militias.

From this context, a plausible sketch of the new advisory unit clearly emerges. Given the past experiences of Hezbollah trainers in Iraq, Yemen, and Syria, the advisors now in Iraq have developed a solid idea on how to train militias for more conventional fighting in a timely and effective manner and direct the integration of their efforts with those of other forces. In this case, they are also stepping into an existing militia infrastructure with which they have familiarity both in the camp and the field, which can streamline the process.

The advisors are probably a mix of Unit 3800 personnel, ESO members, and experienced fighters and special operators previously deployed to Syria. Based on reports that the advisors are already engaged in intelligence operations against ISIS, it is more than likely that a particularly sizeable portion of the advisors are special operations and intelligence personnel, expected to fill capability gaps of Iraqi Shi'a militias.

While significant extension into Iraq does pose a challenge for Hezbollah – which concurrently needs to maintain a strong presence in Lebanon, maintain the momentum of its operations in Syria, and increasingly fill the gap in Syria left by departing Iraqi Shi'a militias – there are reasons to believe that the number of advisors (250) should be considered a conservative estimate. Reports of younger Hezbollah fighters in Syria indicates that in its effort to reconfigure forces for operations in both Syria and extension into Iraq, Hezbollah is likely sending its more experienced fighters from Syria to support the vital force integration effort in Iraq and attempting to backfill the vacuum they have left in Syria with newer fighters.

On July 31, a Reuters report indicated that Ibrahim al-Hajj, a Hezbollah commander and technical specialist with ties to Hassan Nasrallah, was killed in Iraq on July 29. Initially, Lebanese news site Naharnet reported that al-Hajj had been killed in the Qalamoun region of Syria during a clash with rebel forces which left three other Hezbollah fighters dead. However, on next day – when al-Hajj was buried in his hometown of Qiyla in the Beqaa – an ISIS-supporter

Twitter account claimed that al-Hajj had actually been killed in Samarra. The July 31 Reuters report, citing sources in Lebanon, claimed that al-Hajj had been acting as a trainer and was killed near Mosul. The AP has also reported that al-Hajj was part of the team which infiltrated Israel and kidnapped two Israeli soldiers in July 2006, triggering the 2006 Lebanon war.

While the location of al-Hajj's death remains unconfirmed, his public burial and the initial claim that he died fighting in Syria bears striking resemblance to the burials of early Hezbollah casualties in Syria. Those "martyrs" were supposedly killed doing their "jihadist duties," which was intended to obscure the manner and location of their deaths; al-Hajj's death has been described in the same terms by Hezbollah's Al-Manar TV station. In this case, claiming that al-Hajj died in Syria would provide a plausible narrative for his demise while also masking the possibility of his deployment to Iraq.

Both the supposed number of advisors and the murky circumstances surrounding the death of al-Hajj would fit a pattern of Hezbollah's initial foray into a conflict being intentionally understated, as it was in Syria during 2011 and 2012. While Hezbollah's early public messaging on the crisis in Iraq was quite guarded, it eventually did progress to Hassan Nasrallah being quoted as saying on June 17 *"We are ready to sacrifice martyrs in Iraq five times more than what we sacrificed in Syria, in order to protect shrines."*

Also, in Nasrallah's Quds [Jerusalem] Day address on July 25 he denounced ISIS saying *"This is the most dangerous phase since the occupation of Palestine because there is a systematic destruction of countries, peoples, armies and societies … Iraq has entered into a dark tunnel in the name of Islam, unfortunately … Our duty as Muslims today is to condemn what Christians and Muslims are facing in Iraq."* It is reasonable to suspect that Hezbollah is already doing more rather than less in Iraq. Hezbollah activity in Iraq is likely to serve as a force multiplier for Iraqi Shi'a militias, making their activity more effective, but at the possible cost of galvanizing Iraqi Sunni resistance against the government. Furthermore, if Hezbollah's commitment to Iraq truly is more than significant than advertised, the increasing attacks it is facing from Syrian rebels may begin to constitute a rising risk to the continued success of its operations in Syria. How these challenges are balanced, supported, and coordinated with other actors across multiple fronts will remain an area to watch.

Ali Mussa Daqduq

Ali Mussa Daqduq joined Lebanese Hezbollah, shortly after which he was appointed to command a Hezbollah Special Operations unit (Department 2800) in Lebanon. Moving quickly up the ranks, he coordinated operations in large sectors of Lebanon and was also responsible for coordinating the personal security of Lebanese Hezbollah leader Hassan Nasrallah. Ali Mussa Daqduq was a key figure among the Iranian-backed Special Groups in Iraq. Through Iranian sponsorship of Iraqi paramilitary proxies, the Iranian Revolutionary Guard Corps - Quds Force (IRGC-QF) sought to replicate the model used by Lebanese Hezbollah and began training Iraqis in groups of 20 – 60 to function as a unit, or "special group."

Daqduq was sent to Iran with Yussef Hashim, a fellow Lebanese Hezbollah member and head of their Special Operations in Iraq, to train these Iraqi Special Groups and organize them according to a Hezbollah-style structure. During his time in Iran, Daqduq was in contact with Quds Force Commander Qassem Soleimani as well as his Deputy Commander and head of the Department of External Special Operations Hajji Yussef, acting as a key conduit between Lebanese Hezbollah and Iran. Soleimani and Yussef, also known as Abdul Reza Shalai, has been linked to the October 2011 plot to assassinate the Saudi ambassador to the United States in Washington, DC.

IRGC-QF instructed Daqduq to make trips in and out of Iraq to report on the training and operations of the Iraqi Special Groups. Daqduq made four such trips to Iraq in 2006. He monitored and reported on the training and arming of special groups in mortars and rockets, manufacturing and employing IEDs, and kidnapping operations.

In June 2006 IRGC-QF appointed Qais al-Khazali as the head of Special Groups in Iraq. At the time, Khazali was the commander of Asa'ib Ahl al-Haq (AAH), an Iranian-backed militia group that he founded in 2006 following a split from Moqtada al-Sadr and his Jaysh al-Mahdi (JAM) over a challenge for leadership of the Sadr movement and its militant wing. Daqduq was named his chief advisor and served as a liaison between the IRGC-QF and the Special Groups under Khazali's leadership.

In January 20, 2007 AAH gunmen with American-looking uniforms, vehicles and identification cards successfully attacked the Karbala Provincial Joint Coordination Center (PJCC) where U.S. and Iraqi officials were holding a meeting. The gunmen killed five U.S. soldiers and wounded three more in the well-planned and executed attack, which was purportedly orchestrated by Daqduq.

In March 20, 2007, Intelligence gathered from the attack ultimately led to the capture of Qais al-Khazali, his brother Laith al-Khazali, and Daqduq in Basra. When he was captured, Daqduq had detailed documents that discussed tactics to attack Iraqi and coalition forces. He also had a personal journal that showed his involvement with extremist operations in Iraq and meetings with special group members who were targeting other Iraqis and coalition forces in the Diyala province using IEDs, as well as small-arms fire.

In March 2009 Reports revealed that AAH and the Iraqi government were involved in negotiations aimed at bringing the militant group into the political process. The negotiations included discussions on a phased release of hostages being held by AAH in exchange for the release of top AAH members being held in U.S. custody. In June 2009 Laith al-Khazali was transferred from U.S. to Iraqi custody and subsequently released. In December 2009 Qais al-Khazali was transferred from U.S. to Iraqi custody. In January 5, 2010 Qais al-Khazali was released, and traveled to Qom, Iran shortly thereafter.

In December 17, 2011, Daqduq was transferred to Iraqi custody, a move that sparked political controversy in the U.S. as many politicians feared that he would only face minor criminal charges in an Iraqi court. According to Lebanese news reports, a delegation of Lebanese Hezbollah members visited Iraq to meet with high-ranking members of the government to discuss Daqduq's release. In January 3, 2012 Military prosecutors prepared a charge sheet accusing Daqduq of crimes including murder, perfidy, terrorism, and espionage. Brigadier General Mark S. Martins, the chief prosecutor of the commissions system, was to approve the charges; Vice Admiral Bruce MacDonald, the official in charge of the U.S. military commissions, would decide which charges to refer for trial. In the same month, Commander Patrick J. Flor of the Navy was assigned to represent Daqduq. He requested permission from the Pentagon to visit Daqduq in Iraq and view the evidence, but has not received a response.

In February 23, 2012 the charges against Daqduq were revealed publicly. The U.S. military refused to comment on whether the U.S. was actively seeking Daqduq's extradition. In April 2012 Moqtada al-Sadr sent a three-man delegation, led by Awn al-Nabi al-Musawi, to visit Ali Mussa Dadquq at the Baghdad prison at which he was being detained. The aim of the visit was reportedly to check on Dadquq's health and to inform him that the Sadrist Movement was working diligently to achieve his release. In May 7, 2012 a judge at the Central Criminal Court in Baghdad acquitted Daqduq on the grounds of lack of evidence and ordered his release.

Daqduq's lawyer, Abdul-Mahdi al-Mitairi, a Sadrist and former Minister of State in Prime Minister Nouri al-Maliki's second government, said that under Iraqi law the verdict would be appealed immediately, with the verdict of the appeal announced in no more than six months. Hezbollah sources in Beirut insisted that Daqduq would not face any further charges. US military officials maintained that during his time in US custody, Daqduq had confessed freely to the killing of the five American soldiers without being subject to harsh treatment. However, under the Iraqi judicial system, evidence must be collected by an investigating judge: evidence collected by a foreign military force is inadmissible.

A memo approved by Deputy National Security Advisor Denis McDonough read: *"Daqduq should be held accountable for his crimes.While we strongly oppose his acquittal, protections for the accused are built into all judicial systems, including our own. We transferred Daqduq to Iraqi custody out of respect for, and obligation to, the rule of law in Iraq, and while we disagree with this decision, we respect the independence of the Iraqi judiciary. We will continue to work closely with the Iraqi government to explore all legal options to pursue justice in this case."*

Although the exact date of the appeal is unclear, the United States requested extradition for Daqduq. Prime Minister Maliki later denied ever receiving a formal extradition request from the United States. Earlier, two Iraqi courts, including the country's Central Criminal Court, had cleared Daqduq of all charges against him, including involvement in the Karbala attack. The courts cited lack of sufficient, legal evidence that would justify keeping Daqduq in custody. Abdulalmehdi al-Mutiri, Daqduq's lawyer, added that Daqduq remained under Iraqi jurisdiction, and not that of the US. In June 27, 2012

Moqtada al-Sadr called on the Iraqi government to release Daqduq immediately.

In July 12 2012 Antony J. Blinken, the national security adviser to Vice President Joe Biden, announced the Obama Administration's request for Iraq's highest Appeals Court to review and correct its decision to release Daqduq. In August 2, 2012: An Iraqi Court denied the United States' extradition request for Daqduq. The Court explained that it rejected the request because charges against Daqduq had already been dropped. The U.S Embassy in Baghdad declined to comment.

In November 16, 2012 Daqduq was allowed to leave the heavily fortified Green Zone in Baghdad, where he had been under house arrest. Daqduq's lawyer, Abdulalmehdi al-Mutiri, announced that there were no longer any reasons for Daqduq to remain in detention. Daqduq travelled to Beirut shortly after his release. State Department spokesman Victoria Nuland insisted that the United States would continue to pursue all legal means to see that Daqduq sees justice for his crimes. An Iraqi Court acquitted Daqduq of charges of killing American troops, terrorism and espionage.

Ramazan Corps

Iran began to extend its influence in Iraq immediately after the fall of Saddam Hussein's regime in April 2003. Through the Qods Force, Iran's external wing of the Revolutionary Guards Corps, Iran immediately moved money, weapons, and operatives inside Iraq to influence the various fractured Shia political parties and militias.

Iran worked through various militias such as the Mahdi Army, the Badr Corps, the Qazali Network, the Sheibani Network, and a host of other surrogates to attack Coalition forces, Iraqi Security Forces, and rival political leaders. When groups like the Badr Corps and its political backer the Supreme Council for Islamic Revolution in Iraq broke from the Iranian sphere of influence and integrated with the government, the Iranian-backed militias, which have since been designated the Special Groups, began attacking them as well. To streamline operations in Iraq, the Qods Force established a unified command, called the Ramazan Corps, and split Iraq into three roughly geographical regions.

The picture of Qods Force's command structure and operations in Iraq became clearer since US forces began heavily targeting the Iranian networks in late December 2006. Several high-level Qods Force officers – including Qais Qazali, Azhar al Dulaimi, Ali Mussa Daqduq, and Mahmud Farhadi – have been killed or captured in Irbil, Baghdad, and several unnamed locations.

During these raids, Coalition forces seized computers and computer drives, documentation, journals, and other evidence that reinforced information obtained through the interrogations of the Qods Force officers. While military and intelligence sources would not discuss other methods, communications intercepts and satellite imagery are also likely to play a key role in understanding the Qods Force's activities in Iraq.

Critical information about the structure of the Ramazan Corps comes from the Iranian operatives captured in Iraq. Qais Qazali was the leader of the Qazali Network, which was responsible for several high-profile attacks on US and Iraqi forces. Qais, along with his brother Laith Qazali, and several other members of the Qazali Network were captured in early 2007. Azhar al Dulaimi, also a member of the Qazali network, was the tactical commander behind the attack on the Karbala Provincial Joint Coordination Center, which resulted in the kidnapping and subsequent murder of five US soldiers. Ali Mussa Daqduq, who served as the chief of guard to Hezbollah leader Hassan Nasrallah and was the commander of Hezbollah's special forces, was tasked by Iran to organize the Special Groups and "rogue" Mahdi Army cells along the lines of Lebanese Hezbollah. Mahmud Farhadi was the Qods Force officer in charge of the Zafr Command, one of the three units subordinate to the Ramazan Corps.

The Ramazan Corps is split into three separate commands – Nasr, Zafar, and Fajr – each covering a roughly geographical area in Iraq.

The Nasr Command is based in Marivan in the Iranian north and deals with operations in the Kurdish regions and portions of Diyala province. The Zafar Command is based in Mehran in central Iran, and deals with operations in central Iraq, including Baghdad, Najaf, Karbala, Babil, Wasit, and portions of Diyala province.

The Fajr Command is based in Ahvaz in the south and directs operations in Basrah, Dhi Qhar, Maysan, and Muthanna. Inside Iraq, the city of Amarah in Maysan province serves as a Qods Force / Ramazan Corps command and control center as well as one of the major distribution points for weapons in southern Iraq.

The Ramazan Corps' operations begin inside Iran and flow through several points of entry along the border to destinations inside Iraq. Once inside Iraq, weapons are stockpiled and then distributed to local cells to conduct attacks on the primary and secondary targets of opportunity.

Inside Iran, Qods Force manufactures and distributes weapons, provides training for Iraqi recruits, then facilitates the movement of weapons and fighters inside Iraq. Iraqi recruits, largely radicalized Shia from Muqtada al Sadr's Mahdi Army, are sent to Iran for what one US military officer described as "basic jihadi training." The recruits receive several weeks of training with small arms and, depending on the units assigned, mortars and the use of explosively formed penetrators, or EFPs. Several US military sources stated the EFPs are indeed "manufactured" inside Iran at "production lines" in the Iranian hubs of Ahvaz and Mehran. One officer stated the EFPs should not be considered IEDs, as they are professionally manufactured landmines.

In the south and center, recruits and weapons are smuggled through four points of entry. In the central regions, the Mehran point of entry in the central province of Wasit is controlled by the Zafar Command. This is the primary conduit of Iranian weapons into Baghdad. The Al Sheeb entry at Maysan province and the Majnun and Shalamcheh entry points at Basrah province are fed by the Fajar Command based out of Ahvaz.

After being smuggled through the border crossings, Iranian weapons are moved to what are described as "strategic distribution hubs" in the cities of Badrah, Al Kut, Amarah, Qurnah, and Basrah. From these distribution hubs, weapons stocks are then moved forward to "tactical distribution hubs" in Hillah, Diwaniyah, Al Fajr, Samawah, and Nasiriyah.

After the weapons are moved to the strategic distribution hubs, they are warehoused for later use. From strategic hubs, the weapons are distributed to the tactical distribution hubs. From these tactical hubs, the weapons are then distributed to local cells for attacks on US troops, Iraqi Security Forces, and rival political and militia leaders as needed.

Baghdad is considered strategic center of gravity for EFP and mortar strikes. The Iranians believe they can influence events decisively by attacking Coalition and Iraqi targets in and around Baghdad. Iranian-made mortars and larger rockets are fired regularly at the massive Victory complex south of Baghdad where the US military maintains a large presence. US and Iraqi military patrols are targeted by EFPs inside Baghdad.

Khalil Harb

In the years prior to Israel's withdrawal from southern Lebanon in 2000, Khalil Harb served as the deputy commander for Hizballah's central military unit's southern Lebanon region from 1988 to 1992, and as the commander for this region from 1992 to 1994. From 1994 to 1997, Harb served as the commander of Hizballah's central military operations. By 2000, Harb supervised Hizballah military operations inside Israel, Jordan, Cyprus, and Turkey.

In late November 2000, Harb was given responsibility for overseeing work of the Islamic Resistance, including assisting with the smuggling of Hamas and Palestinian Islamic Jihad operatives from Syria into the West Bank via Jordan. By late 2003, Harb was head of the Syrian/Jordan/Israel/Egypt operations unit, which was subordinate to Hizballah's Islamic Jihad council.

In March 2006, Harb served as Hizballah's chief of military liaison with the Palestinian factions and Iran, dealing almost exclusively with Palestinians and Iranians inside and outside the territories. Prior to this posting, Harb had served as Hizballah's chief of military special operations. During the summer of 2006, Harb was given command of a Hizballah special operations unit in southern Lebanon, which engaged the Israeli Defense Forces (IDF) in July 2006, at the Lebanese-Israeli border where IDF Special Forces entered Lebanon. In early 2007, Khalil Harb was chief of Hizballah's Unit 1800, also known as Hizballah's Nun Unit, the Hizballah entity responsible for supporting Palestinian militants and conducting Hizballah operations in the countries surrounding Israel, and he travelled to Iran for meetings regarding coordination between Hizballah, Iran, and the Palestinians.

In February 2010, Harb, serving as the leader of the Palestinian activities for Hizballah, planned unspecified attacks against Israeli officials in Israel, in retaliation for the assassination of former Hizballah External Security Organization (ESO) chief Imad Mughniyah. By mid-May 2010, Hizballah created a new position for Harb as "advisor to the Secretary General," which provided Harb oversight of Hizballah Unit 1800, which he previously commanded.

As of 2012, Harb was responsible for Hizballah's Yemen activities and was involved in the political side of Hizballah's Yemen portfolio. Harb also served as commander of a Lebanon-based Hizballah special unit that focused on Israel. Since the summer of 2012, Harb has been involved in the movement of large amounts of currency to Yemen, through Saudi Arabia and the U.A.E., and in late 2012, Harb advised the leader of a Yemeni political party that the party's monthly Hizballah funding of $50,000 was ready for pick up.

Muhammad Kawtharani

As the individual in charge of Hizballah's Iraq activities, Kawtharani has worked on behalf of Hizballah's leadership to promote the group's interests in Iraq, including Hizballah efforts to provide training, funding, political, and logistical support to Iraqi Shi'a insurgent groups. A member of Hizballah's Political Council, Kawtharani also helped secure the release from Iraqi custody of Hizballah operative Ali Musa Daqduq, a senior Hizballah commander designated by the Treasury Department in November 2012 who was responsible for numerous attacks against Coalition Force in Iraq, including planning a January 20, 2007 attack on the Karbala Joint Provincial Coordination Center that resulted in the deaths of five U.S. soldiers. Over the last year, Kawtharani has assisted in getting fighters to Syria to support the Assad regime.

Muhammad Yusuf Ahmad Mansur

Muhammad Yusuf Ahmad Mansur (Mansur), a member of Hizballah since at least 1986, once served in a Hizballah military unit operating in south Lebanon. Around 2004, Mansur was transferred to Hizballah's Unit 1800. Mansur was subsequently dispatched to Egypt to work with Unit 1800 under Muhammad Qabalan, and in 2008, the cell escalated its operations to target tourist destinations in Egypt. Mansur served as the Egypt-based cell leader. By early 2009, Egyptian authorities had disrupted the Hizballah cell and arrested and detained Mansur and dozens of other individuals for planning to carry out terrorist operations against Israeli and other tourists in Egypt.

Hizballah Secretary-General Hassan Nasrallah in November 2009 publicly acknowledged that Mansur was a Hizballah member involved in transporting arms and equipment to Palestinian militants. In April 2010, an Egyptian court sentenced Mansur to 15 years for his involvement in the cell, which was subordinate to Hizballah's Unit 1800. However, in late January 2011, the imprisoned members of the Hizballah cell escaped and Mansur returned to Lebanon. In February 2011, Mansur appeared on Lebanese television with Hizballah officials at a Hizballah rally in Beirut.

Muhammad Qabalan

Hizballah cell leader Muhammad Qabalan (Qabalan) once served as the head of a Hizballah infantry platoon. In 2008, Qabalan, as a leader in Hizballah's Unit 1800, was serving as the Lebanon-based head of the Hizballah Egypt-based cell targeting tourist destinations in Egypt and was coordinating the cell's activities from Lebanon. In April 2010, an Egyptian court sentenced Qabalan in absentia to life imprisonment for his involvement in the cell, which was subordinate to Hizballah's Unit 1800. As of late 2011, Qabalan worked in a separate Hizballah covert unit operating in the Middle East.

Abu Mahdi al-Muhandis

Abu Mahdi al-Muhandis is wanted by Kuwaiti and US authorities, as well as by Interpol. Muhandis is accused of the staging attacks on the US and French embassies in Kuwait on 12 December 1983, which killed six people and injured another 80, including citizens of western countries. An investigation conducted jointly by the Kuwaiti and US authorities at the time reportedly uncovered evidence of Muhandis' involvement, along with 17 others from the Dawa Party, in these attacks.

Muhandis and his comrades were sentenced to death but he managed to flee Kuwait to Iran using a fake Pakistani passport. He was blacklisted in the Gulf countries, Egypt and the Arab Maghreb, in Europe and the US. He has spent the past ten years in Iran, Syria and Iraq. Today, Muhandis holds a high-ranking position in Baghdad, with extensive prerogatives not even enjoyed by the three deputies of the president or the speaker of parliament.

Muhandis is the vice-president of the Popular Mobilisation militia (al-Hashd al-Shaabi) affiliated with the Iraqi Council of Ministers, a group composed of some 42 local militias and some 70,000 fighters. In a press conference held in the Green Zone on Thursday, 1 January 2015, Muhandis' first ever press conference, he described himself as a military commander and a defector from the Iranian Revolutionary Guards corps. Muhandis' appearance in a press conference at the heart of the Green Zone came as a surprise to many, as his name has always been linked to brutal sectarian crimes.

He purportedly appeared in several video clips appearing to execute Iraqi soldiers taken captive by the Iranian Army in 1985, during the Iran-Iraq war. After the Gulf countries backed Iraq in its war with Tehran, Muhandis is understood to have [attacked] various targets in Kuwait.

According to Iraqi security reports and documents, Abu Mahdi al-Muhandis was born in 1954 as Jamal Jaafar Ibrahim, son to an Iraqi father and an Iranian mother in Basra. He pursued his studies at the Faculty of Engineering in 1977 and joined the Dawa Party the same year. He left Iraq for Kuwait in 1979, after former Iraqi President Saddam Hussein assumed power and banned all religious parties in the country. Muhandis settled in Kuwait for several years. According to the reports, in Kuwait he was involved in anti-Saddam activity before he was banned from this work by the Kuwaiti government.

After the Gulf countries backed Iraq in its war on Tehran, Muhandis is understood to have retaliated by attacking various targets in Kuwait, including the US and French embassies. The Kuwaiti judiciary convicted Muhandis and sentenced him to death. But Muhandis had already left the country. He fled to Iran by sea a few hours after the attacks. He is understood to have settled in Iran and married an Iranian woman a few years older than him, becoming an Iranian citizen - and subsequently being appointed as a military adviser to al-Quds Corps, tasked with attacking Iraqi forces deployed in Basra, his hometown.

In 1985, the Kuwaiti general prosecutor officially charged him of involvement in an assassination attempt on the late Emir Jabir al-Ahmad. Ever since that time, he has been Kuwait's most wanted fugitive, and on the US blacklist. His name even appeared on the "most wanted" list before that of Osama Bin Laden, al-Qaeda's former leader, for a time.

In 1987, Muhandis was officially appointed leader of the Badr organisation, a Shia militia group in Iran. A few years later, he was active in al-Tajjamou al-Islami, a group affiliated with al-Quds Corps. He joined Iranian forces in attacks on Iraqi towns in early 1988, attacks that left hundreds of Iraqi soldiers and civilians dead.

In March 2003, after US troops entered Iraq, Muhandis appeared under the name Jamal al-Ibrahimi and ran in the 2005 parliamentary elections. He joined the Dawa Party's electoral list, headed by former Iraqi Prime Minister Nouri al-Maliki, and won a seat in Babel governorate.

A force of US marines stormed his residence in east Baghdad after his true identity was revealed, but he managed to flee again to Iran after spending several months hiding and being pursued by the US. He only re-entered Iraq when the US forces pulled out in 2010, on short visits.